MR. WEBSTER'S ADDRESS

AT THE

LAYING OF THE CORNER STONE

OF THE

ADDITION TO THE CAPITOL;

JULY 4TH, 1851.

"STET CAPITOLIUM
FULGENS;
LATE NOMEN IN ULTIMAS
EXTENDAT ORAS."

WASHINGTON:
GIDEON AND CO., PRINTERS.
1851.

ADDRESS.

Fellow-Citizens: I congratulate you, I give you joy, on the return of this Anniversary; and I felicitate you, also, on the more particular purpose of which this ever-memorable day has been chosen to witness the fulfilment. Hail! all hail! I see before and around me a mass of faces, glowing with cheerfulness and patriotic pride. I see thousands of eyes, turned towards other eyes, all sparkling with gratification and delight. This is the New World! This is America! This is Washington! and this the Capitol of the United States! And where else, among the Nations, can the seat of government be surrounded, on any day of any year, by those who have more reason to rejoice in the blessings which they possess? Nowhere, fellow-citizens; assuredly, nowhere. Let us, then, meet this rising sun with joy and thanksgiving!

This is that day of the year which announced to mankind the great fact of American Independence. This fresh and brilliant morning blesses our vision with another beholding of the Birthday of our Nation; and we see that nation, of recent origin, now among the most considerable and powerful, and spreading over the continent from sea to sea.

Among the first colonists from Europe to this part of America, there were some, doubtless, who contemplated the distant consequences of their undertaking, and who saw a great futurity; but, in general, their hopes were limited to the enjoyment of a safe asylum from tyranny, religious and civil, and to respectable subsistence, by industry and toil. A thick veil hid our times from their view. But the progress of America, however slow, could not but at length awaken genius, and attract the attention of mankind.

In the early part of the next century, Bishop Berkeley, who, it will be remembered, had resided for some time in Newport, in Rhode Island, wrote his well-known "Verses on the Prospect of planting ARTS and LEARNING in AMERICA." The last stanza of this little Poem seems to have been produced by a high poetical inspiration:

> "Westward the course of empire takes its way;
> The four first acts already past,
> A fifth shall close the drama with the day:
> Time's noblest offspring is the last."

This extraordinary prophecy may be considered only as the result of long foresight and uncommon sagacity; of a foresight and sagacity stimulated, nevertheless, by excited feeling and high enthusiasm. So clear a vision of what America would become was not founded on square miles, or on existing numbers, or on any vulgar laws of statistics. It was an intuitive glance into futurity; it was a grand conception, strong, ardent, glowing, embracing all time since the creation of the world, and all regions of which that world is composed; and judging of the future by just analogy with the past. And the inimitable imagery and beauty with which the thought is expressed, joined to the conception itself, render it one of the most striking passages in our language.

On the day of the declaration of Independence our illustrious fathers performed the first scene in the last great act of this drama; one, in real importance, infinitely exceeding that for which the great English poet invoked.

> "A muse of fire,
> A kingdom for a stage, princes to act,
> And monarchs to behold the swelling scene!"

The Muse inspiring our Fathers was the Genius of Liberty, all on fire with a sense of oppression, and a resolution to throw it off; the whole world was the stage, and higher characters than princes trod it; and, instead of monarchs, countries and nations and the age beheld the swelling scene. How well the characters were cast, and how well each acted his part, and what emotions the whole performance excited, let history, now and hereafter, tell.

At a subsequent period, but before the declaration of Independence, the Bishop of St. Asaph published a Discourse, in which the following remarkable passages are found:

"It is difficult for man to look into the destiny of future ages; 'the designs of Providence are too vast and complicated, and our 'own powers are too narrow to admit of much satisfaction to our 'curiosity. But, when we see many great and powerful causes 'constantly at work, we cannot doubt of their producing propor-'tionable effects.

"The colonies in North America have not only taken root and 'acquired strength, *but seem hastening with an accelerated progress 'to such a powerful State as may introduce a new and important 'change in human affairs.*

"Descended from ancestors of the most improved and enlight-'ened part of the old world, they receive, as it were by inherit-'ance, all the improvements and discoveries of their mother 'country. And it happens fortunately for them to commence 'their flourishing State at a time when the human understanding 'has attained to the free use of its powers, and has learned to act 'with vigor and certainty. They may avail themselves not only 'of the experience and industry, but even of the errors and mis-'takes of former days. Let it be considered for how many ages 'a great part of the world appears not to have thought at all; 'how many more they have been busied in forming systems and 'conjectures, while reason has been lost in a labyrinth of words, 'and they never seem to have suspected on what frivolous matters 'their minds were employed.

"And let it be well understood what rapid improvements, what 'important discoveries have been made, in a few years, by a few 'countries, with our own at their head, which have at last dis-'covered the right method of using their faculties.

"May we not reasonably expect that a number of provinces, 'possessed of these advantages, and quickened by mutual emula-'tion, with only the common progress of the human mind, should 'very considerably enlarge the boundaries of science?

"The vast continent itself, over which they are gradually 'spreading, may be considered as a treasure yet untouched of 'natural productions that shall hereafter afford ample matter for 'commerce and contemplation. And, if we reflect what a stock 'of knowledge may be accumulated by the constant progress of 'industry and observation, fed with fresh supplies from the stores 'of nature, assisted sometimes by those happy strokes of chance 'which mock all the powers of invention, and sometimes by those 'superior characters which arise occasionally to instruct and en-

'lighten the world, it is difficult even to imagine to what height 'of improvement their discoveries may extend.

"*And perhaps they may make as considerable advances in the 'arts of civil government and the conduct of life.* We have reason 'to be proud, and even jealous, of our excellent constitution; but 'those equitable principles on which it was formed, an equal re-'presentation, (the best discovery of political wisdom,) and a just 'and commodious distribution of power, which with us were the 'price of civil wars, and the rewards of the virtues and sufferings 'of our ancestors, descend to them as a natural inheritance, with-'out toil or pain.

"*But must they rest here, as in the utmost effort of human genius? 'Can chance and time, the wisdom and the experience of public men, 'suggest no new remedy against the evils* which vices and ambition 'are perpetually apt to cause? May they not hope, without pre-'sumption, to preserve a greater zeal for piety and public devo-'tion than we have done? For sure it can hardly happen to them, 'as it has to us, that when religion is best understood and ren-'dered most pure and reasonable, that then should be the precise 'time when many cease to believe and practice it, and all in 'general become most indifferent to it?.

"May they not possibly be more successful than their mother 'country has been in preserving that reverence and authority 'which is due to the laws? to those who make, and to those who 'execute them? *May not a method be invented of procuring some 'tolerable share of the comforts of life to those inferior useful ranks 'of men to whose industry we are indebted for the whole? Time 'and discipline may discover some means to correct the extreme in-'equalities of condition between the rich and the poor, so dangerous 'to the innocence and happiness of both.* They may fortunately be 'led by habit and choice to despise that luxury which is consid-'ered with us the true enjoyment of wealth. They may have 'little relish for that ceaseless hurry of amusements which is pur-'sued in this country without pleasure, exercise, or employment. 'And perhaps, after trying some of our follies and caprices and 'rejecting the rest, they may be led by reason and experiment to 'that old simplicity which was first pointed out by Nature, and 'has produced those models which we still admire in arts, elo-'quence, and manners. *The diversity of new scenes and situations,* '*which so many growing States must necessarily pass through, may* '*introduce changes in the fluctuating opinions and manners of men* '*which we can form no conception of;* and not only the gracious 'disposition of Providence, but the visible preparation of causes, 'seems to indicate strong tendencies towards a general improve-'ment."

Fellow-citizens, this "gracious disposition of Providence," and this "visible preparation of causes," at length brought on the hour for decisive action. On the 4th of July, 1776, the Representatives of the United States of America in Congress assembled declared that these United Colonies are, and of right ought to be, FREE AND INDEPENDENT STATES.

This declaration, made by most patriotic and resolute men, trusting in the justice of their cause and the protection of Heaven, and yet made not without deep solicitude and anxiety, has now stood for seventy-five years, and still stands. It was sealed in blood. It has met dangers, and overcome them; it has had enemies, and conquered them; it has had detractors, and abashed them all; it has had doubting friends, but it has cleared all doubts away; and now, to-day, raising its august form higher than the clouds, twenty millions of people contemplate it with hallowed love, and the world beholds it, and the consequences which have followed from it, with profound admiration.

This anniversary animates, and gladdens, and unites all American hearts. On other days of the year we may be party men, indulging in controversies, more or less important to the public good; we may have likes and dislikes, and we may maintain our political differences, often with warm, and sometimes with angry feelings. But to-day, we are Americans all; and all nothing but Americans. As the great luminary over our heads, dissipating mists and fogs, now cheers the whole hemisphere, so do the associations connected with this day disperse all cloudy and sullen weather in the minds and hearts of true Americans. Every man's heart swells within him; every man's port and bearing becomes somewhat more proud and lofty, as he remembers that seventy-five years have rolled away, and that the great inheritance of liberty is still his: his, undiminished and unimpaired; his in all its original glory; his to enjoy; his to protect; and his to transmit to future generations.

Fellow-citizens: This inheritance which we enjoy to-day is not only an inheritance of liberty, but of our own peculiar American liberty. Liberty has existed in other times, in other countries, and in other forms. There has been a Grecian liberty, bold and powerful, full of spirit, eloquence, and fire; a liberty which produced multitudes of great men, and has transmitted one immortal name, the name of Demosthenes, to posterity. But still it was a liberty of disconnected States, sometimes united, indeed, by temporary leagues and confederacies, but often involved in wars between themselves. The sword of Sparta turned its sharpest edge against Athens, enslaved her, and devastated Greece; and, in her turn, Sparta was compelled to bend before the power of Thebes. And let it ever be remembered, especially let the truth sink deep into all American minds, that it was the WANT OF UNION among her several States which finally gave the mastery of all Greece to Philip of Macedon.

And there has also been a Roman liberty, a proud, ambitious, domineering spirit, professing free and popular principles in Rome itself, but, even in the best days of the Republic, ready to carry slavery and chains into her provinces, and through every country over which her eagles could be borne. What was the liberty of Spain, or Gaul, or Germany, or Britain in the days of Rome? Did true constitutional liberty then exist? As the Roman Empire declined, her provinces, not instructed in the principles of free popular government, one after another declined also, and when Rome herself fell in the end, all fell together.

I have said, gentlemen, that our inheritance is an inheritance of American liberty. That liberty is characteristic, peculiar, and altogether our own. Nothing like it existed in former times, nor was known in the most enlightened States of antiquity; while with us its principles have become interwoven into the minds of individual men, connected with our daily opinions, and our daily habits, until it is, if I may so say, an element of social as well as of political life; and the consequence is, that to whatever region an American citizen carries himself, he takes with him, fully developed in his own understanding and experience, our American principles and opinions, and becomes ready at once, in co-operation with others, to apply them to the formation of new Governments. Of this a most wonderful instance may be seen in the history of the State of California.

On a former occasion I have ventured to remark that, "It is 'very difficult to establish a free conservative Government for 'the equal advancement of all the interests of society. What 'has Germany done; learned Germany, fuller of ancient lore than 'all the world beside? What has Italy done? What have they 'done who dwell on the spot where Cicero lived? They have 'not the power of self-government which a common town-meet-'ing, with us, possesses?" "Yes, I say, that those persons who 'have gone from our town-meetings to dig gold in California, are 'more fit to make a Republican Government than any body of 'men in Germany or Italy; because they have learned this one 'great lesson, that there is no security without law, and that, 'under the circumstances in which they are placed, where there 'is no military authority to cut their throats, there is no sovereign 'will but the will of the majority; that, therefore, if they remain, 'they must submit to that will." And this I believe to be strictly true.

Now, fellow-citizens, if your patience will hold out, I will venture, before proceeding to the more appropriate and particular duties of the day, to state, in a few words, what I take these American political principles in substance to be. They consist, as I think, in the first place, in the establishment of popular Governments, on the basis of representation; for it is plain that a pure democracy, like that which existed in some of the States of Greece, in which every individual had a direct vote in the enactment of all laws, cannot possibly exist in a country of wide extent. This representation is to be made as equal as circumstances will allow. Now, this principle of popular representation, prevailing either in all the branches of Governments, or in some of them, has existed in these States almost from the days of the settlements at Jamestown and Plymouth; borrowed, no doubt, from the example of the popular branch of the British Legislature. The representation of the people in the British House of Commons was, indeed, originally very unequal, and is yet not equal. Indeed, it may be doubted whether the appearance of Knights and Burgesses assembling on the summons of the Crown, was not intended at first as an assistance and support to the Royal prerogative, in matters of revenue and taxation, rather than as a mode of ascertaining popular opinion. Nevertheless, representa-

tion had a popular origin, and savored more and more of the character of that origin, as it acquired, by slow degrees, greater and greater strength, in the actual government of the country. In fact, the constitution of the House of Commons was a form of representation, however unequal; numbers were counted, and majorities prevailed; and when our ancestors, acting upon this example, introduced more equality of representation, the idea assumed a more rational and distinct shape. At any rate, this manner of exercising popular power was familiar to our fathers when they settled on this continent. They adopted it, and generation has risen up after generation, all acknowledging it, and becoming acquainted with its practice and its forms.

And the next fundamental principle in our system is, that the will of the majority, fairly expressed through the means of representation, shall have the force of law; and it is quite evident that in a country without Thrones or Aristocracies or privileged castes or classes, there can be no other foundation for law to stand upon.

And, as the necessary result of this, the third element is, that the law is the supreme rule for the government of all. The great sentiment of Alcæus, so beautifully presented to us by Sir William Jones, is absolutely indispensable to the construction and maintenance of our political systems:

"What constitutes a State?
Not high rais'd battlements or labored mound,
Thick wall or moated gate;
Not cities proud, with spires and turrets crown'd;
Not bays and broad arm'd ports,
Where, laughing at the storm, rich navies ride;
Not starr'd and spangled courts,
Where low-brow'd baseness wafts perfume to pride.
No—MEN, high-minded MEN,
With powers as far above dull brutes endued
In forests, brake or den,
As beasts excel cold rock and brambles rude:
Men who their duties know,
But know their rights, and knowing, dare maintain;
Prevent the long-aim'd blow,
And crush the tyrant while they rend the chain:
These constitute a State;
And SOVEREIGN LAW, that State's collected will,
O'er thrones and globes elate
Sits empress, crowning good, repressing ill."

And, finally, another most important part of the great fabric of American liberty is, that there shall be written constitutions, founded on the immediate authority of the people themselves, and regulating and restraining all the powers conferred upon Government, whether legislative, executive, or judicial.

This, fellow-citizens, I suppose to be a just summary of our American principles, and I have on this occasion sought to express them in the plainest and in the fewest words. The summary may not be entirely exact, but I hope it may be sufficiently so to make manifest to the rising generation among ourselves, and to those elsewhere, who may choose to inquire into the nature of our political institutions, the general theory upon which they are founded. And I now proceed to add, that the strong and deep-settled conviction of all intelligent persons amongst us is, that in order to support a useful and wise Government upon these popular principles, the general education of the people, and the wide diffusion of pure morality and true religion, are indispensable. Individual virtue is a part of public virtue. It is difficult to conceive how there can remain morality in the Government when it shall cease to exist among the people; or how the aggregate of the political institutions, all the organs of which consist only of men, should be wise, and beneficent, and competent to inspire confidence, if the opposite qualities belong to the individuals who constitute those organs, and make up that aggregate.

And now, fellow-citizens, I take leave of this part of the duty which I proposed to perform, and once more felicitating you and myself that our eyes have seen the light of this blessed morning, and that our ears have heard the shouts with which joyous thousands welcome its return, and joining with you in the hope that every revolving year shall renew these rejoicings to the end of time, I proceed to address you, shortly, upon the particular occasion of our assembling here to-day.

Fellow-citizens, by the act of Congress of 30th September, 1850, provision was made for the Extension of the Capitol, according to such plan as might be approved by the President of the United States, and the necessary sums to be expended, under his direction, by such architect as he might appoint. This measure was imperatively demanded for the use of the Legislative and Judiciary departments, the public libraries, the occasional accommodation of the Chief Executive Magistrate, and for other objects. No act of Congress incurring a large expenditure has received more general approbation from the people. The President has proceeded to execute this law. He has approved a plan; he has appointed an architect; and all things are now ready for the commencement of the work.

The Anniversary of National Independence appeared to afford an auspicious occasion for laying the foundation-stone of the additional building. That ceremony has now been performed, by the President himself, in the presence and view of this multitude. He has thought that the day and the occasion made a united and imperative call for some short address to the people here assembled; and it is at his request that I have appeared before you to perform that part of the duty which was deemed incumbent on us.

Beneath the stone is deposited, among other things, a list of which will be published, the following brief account of the proceedings of this day, in my handwriting:

"On the morning of the first day of the Seventy-sixth year of 'the Independence of the United States of America, in the City of 'Washington, being the 4th day of July, 1851, this stone, designed 'as the corner-stone of the extension of the Capitol, according to 'a plan approved by the President, in pursuance of an act of Con- 'gress, was laid by

'MILLARD FILLMORE,

'PRESIDENT OF THE UNITED STATES,

'assisted by the Grand Master of the Masonic Lodges, in 'the presence of many members of Congress, of officers of the 'Executive and Judiciary Departments, National, State, and 'District, of officers of the army and navy, the Corporate autho- 'rities of this and neighboring cities, many associations, civil and 'military and masonic, officers of the Smithsonian Institution and 'National Institute, professors of colleges and teachers of schools 'of the District, with their students and pupils, and a vast con- 'course of people from places near and remote, including a few 'surviving gentlemen who witnessed the laying of the corner-stone 'of the Capitol by President Washington, on the eighteenth day 'of September, seventeen hundred and ninety-three.

"If, therefore, it shall be hereafter the will of God that this 'structure shall fall from its base, that its foundation be upturned, 'and this deposit brought to the eyes of men, be it then known, 'that, on this day, the Union of the United States of America 'stands firm, that their Constitution still exists unimpaired, and 'with all its original usefulness and glory; growing every day 'stronger and stronger in the affections of the great body of the 'American people, and attracting more and more the admiration 'of the world. And all here assembled, whether belonging to 'public life or to private life, with hearts devoutly thankful to 'Almighty God for the preservation of the liberty and happiness 'of the country, unite in sincere and fervent prayers that this 'deposite, and the walls and arches, the domes and towers, the 'columns and entablatures now to be erected over it may endure 'forever!

"God save the United States of America.

"DANIEL WEBSTER,
"*Secretary of State of the United States.*"

Fellow-citizens: Fifty-eight years ago Washington stood on this spot to execute a duty like that which has now been performed. He then laid the corner-stone of the original Capitol. He was at the head of the Government, at that time weak in resources, burdened with debt, just struggling into political existence and respectability, and agitated by the heaving waves which were overturning European thrones. But even then, in many important respects, the Government was strong. It was strong in Washington's own great character; it was strong in the wisdom and patriotism of other eminent public men, his political associates and fellow-laborers; and it was strong in the affections of the people.

Since that time astonishing changes have been wrought in the condition and prospects of the American People; and a degree of progress witnessed with which the world can furnish no parallel. As we review the course of that progress, wonder and amazement arrest our attention at every step. The present occasion, although allowing of no lengthened remarks, may yet perhaps admit of a short comparative statement between important subjects of national interest as they existed at that day and as they now exist. I have adopted for this purpose the tabular form of statement, as being the most brief and the most accurate.

COMPARATIVE TABLE.

	Year 1793.	Year 1851.
Number of States	15	31
Representatives and Senators in Congress	135	295
Population of the United States . . .	3,929,328	23,267,498
Population of Boston	18,038	136,871
Population of Baltimore	13,503	169,054
Population of Philadelphia	42,520	409,045
Population of New York (city) . . .	33,121	515,507
Population of Washington	. . . .	40,075
Population of Richmond	4,000	27,582
Population of Charleston	16,359	42,983
Amount of receipts into the Treasury	$5,720,624	$43,774,848
Amount of expenditures of the U. States	$7,529,575	$39,355,268
Amount of imports	$31,000,000	$178,138,318
Amount of exports	$26,109,000	$151,898,720
Amount of tonnage . . . . (tons)	520,764	3,535,454
Area of the U. States in square miles	805,461	3,314,365
Rank and file of the army	5,120	10,000
Militia (enrolled)	. . . .	2,006,456
Navy of the United States (vessels) .	(none.)	76
Navy armament (ordnance)	. . . .	2,012
Treaties and conventions with foreign Powers	9	90
Light-houses and light-boats	12	372
Expenditures for do.	$12,061	$529,265
Area of the Capitol	one-half acre	$4\frac{1}{3}$ acres.
No. of miles of railroad in operation .	. . . .	10,287
Cost of ditto	. . . .	$306,607,954
No. of miles in course of construction	. . . .	10,092
Lines of telegraph, in miles	. . . .	15,000
Number of post offices	209	21,551
Number of miles of post route . . .	5,642	178,762
Amount of revenue from post offices .	$104,747	$5,592,971
Amount of expenditures of Post Office Department	$72,040	$5,212,953
Number of miles mail transportation .	. . . .	46,541,423
Number colleges	19	121
Public libraries	35	694
Volumes in ditto	75,000	2,201,632
School libraries	. . . .	10,000
Volumes in ditto	. . . .	2,000,000
Emigrants from Europe to the U. S. .	10,000	299,610
Coinage at the Mint	$9,664	$52,019,465

In respect to the growth of Western trade and commerce, I extract a few sentences from a very valuable address before the Historical Society of Ohio, by William D. Gallagher, Esq., 1850:

"A few facts will exhibit as well as a volume the wonderful 'growth of Western trade and commerce. Previous to the year '1800, some eight or ten keel-boats, of twenty or twenty-five tons 'each, performed all the carrying trade between Cincinnati and 'Pittsburg. In 1802 the first Government vessel appeared on 'Lake Erie. In 1811 the first steamboat (the Orleans) was 'launched at Pittsburg. In 1826 the waters of Michigan were 'first ploughed by the keel of a steamboat, a pleasure trip to 'Green Bay being planned and executed in the summer of this 'year. In 1832 a steamboat first appeared at Chicago. At the 'present time the entire number of steamboats running on the 'Mississippi and Ohio, and their tributaries, is more probably over 'than under six hundred; the aggregate tonnage of which is not 'short of one hundred and forty thousand, a larger number of 'steamboats than England can claim, and a greater steam com-'mercial marine than that employed by Great Britain and her 'dependencies."

And now, fellow-citizens, having stated to you this infallible proof of the growth and prosperity of the nation, I ask you, and I would ask every man, whether the Government which has been over us has proved itself an affliction or a curse to the country, or any part of it?

Ye men of the South, of all the original Southern States, what say you to all this? Are you, or any of you, ashamed of this great work of your fathers? Your fathers were not they who stoned the prophets and killed them. They were among the prophets; they were of the prophets; they were themselves the prophets.

Ye men of Virginia, what do you say to all this? Ye men of the Potomac, dwelling along the shores of that river on which WASHINGTON lived, and died, and where his remains now rest, ye, so many of whom may see the domes of the Capitol from your own homes, what say ye?

Ye men of James river and the Bay, places consecrated by the early settlement of your commonwealth, what do you say? Do you desire, from the soil of your State, or as you travel to the

North, to see these halls vacated, their beauty and ornaments destroyed, and their national usefulness clean gone forever?

Ye men beyond the Blue Ridge, many thousands of whom are nearer to this Capitol than to the seat of government of your own State, what do you think of breaking this great association into fragments of States and of People? I know some of you, and I believe you all, would be almost as much shocked at the announcement of such a catastrophe as if you were to be informed that the Blue Ridge itself would soon totter from its base. And ye men of Western Virginia, who occupy the great slope from the top of the Alleghany to the Ohio and Kentucky, what course do you propose to yourselves by disunion? If you "secede," what do you "secede" from, and what do you "accede" to? Do you look for the current of the Ohio to change, and to bring you and your commerce to the tide-waters of Eastern rivers? What man in his senses can suppose that you will remain part and parcel of Virginia a month after Virginia should have ceased to be part and parcel of the United States?

The secession of Virginia! the secession of Virginia, whether alone or in company, is most improbable, the greatest of all improbabilities. Virginia, to her everlasting honor, acted a great part in framing and establishing the present Constitution. She has had her reward and her distinction. Seven of her noble sons have each filled the Presidency, and enjoyed the highest honors of the country. Dolorous complaints come up to us from the South that Virginia will not head the procession of secession, and lead the other Southern States out of the Union. This, if it should happen, would be something of a marvel, certainly, considering how much pains Virginia took to lead these same States into the Union, and considering, too, that she has partaken as largely of its benefits and its government as any other State.

And ye men of the other Southern States, members of the old thirteen; yes, members of the old thirteen; that always touches my regard and my sympathies; North Carolina, Georgia, South Carolina! What page in your history, or in the history of any one of you, is brighter than those which have been recorded since the Union was formed? Or through what effect has your prosperity been greater, or your peace and happiness better secured? What names even has South Carolina, now so much dissatisfied, what names has she of which her intelligent sons are more proud than those which have been connected with the Government of the United States? In revolutionary times, and in the earliest days of this Constitution, there was no State more honored, or more deserving to be honored. Where is she now? And what a fall is there, my countrymen! But I leave her to her own reflections, commending to her, with all my heart, the due consideration of her own example in times now gone by.

Fellow-citizens, there are some diseases of the mind as well as of the body, diseases of communities, as well as diseases of individuals, that must be left to their own cure; at least it is wise to leave them so, until the last critical moment shall arrive.

I hope it is not irreverent, and certainly it is not intended as reproach, when I say, that I know no stronger expression in our language than that which describes the restoration of a wayward son, "he came to himself." He had broken away from all the ties of love, family, and friendship. He had forsaken everything which he had once regarded in his father's house. He had quitted his natural sympathies, affections, and habits, and taken his journey into a far country. He had gone away from himself, and out of himself. But misfortunes overtook him, and famine threatened him with starvation and death. No entreaties from home followed him to beckon him back; no admonition from others warned him of his fate. But the hour of reflection had come, and nature and conscience wrought within him, until at length "he *came* to himself.

And now, ye men of the new States of the South! You are not of the original thirteen. The battle had been fought and won, the revolution achieved, and the Constitution established, before your States had any existence as States. You came to a prepared banquet, and had seats assigned you at table, just as honorable as those which were filled by older guests. You have been and are singularly prosperous; and if any one should deny this, you would at once contradict his assertion. You have bought vast quantities of choice and excellent land at the lowest price; and if the public domain has not been lavished upon you, you yourselves will admit that it has been appropriated to your own uses by a very liberal hand. And yet in some of these States, not in all, persons are found in favor of a dissolution of the Union, or of secession from it. Such opinions are expressed even where the general prosperity of the community has been the most rapidly advanced. In the flourishing and interesting State of Mississippi, for example, there is a large party which insists that her grievances are intolerable, that the whole body politic is in a state of suffering, and all along, and through her whole extent on the Mississippi, a loud cry rings that her only remedy is "secession," "secession." Now, gentlemen, what infliction does the State of Mississippi suffer under? What oppression prostrates her strength or destroys her happiness? Before we can judge of the proper remedy we must know something of the disease; and, for my part, I confess that the real evil existing in the case appears to me to be a certain inquietude, or uneasiness, growing out of a high degree of prosperity and consciousness of wealth and power, which sometimes lead men to be ready for changes, and to push on to still higher elevation. If this be the truth of the matter, her political doctors are about right. If the complaint spring from over-wrought prosperity, for that disease I have no doubt that secession would prove a sovereign remedy.

But I return to the leading topic on which I was engaged. In the department of invention there have been wonderful applications of science to arts within the last sixty years. The spacious hall of the Patent Office is at once the repository and proof of American inventive art and genius. Their results are seen in the numerous improvements by which human labor is abridged.

Without going into details, it may be sufficient to say that many of the applications of steam to locomotion and manufactures; of electricity and magnetism to the production of mechanical motion; the electrical telegraph; the registration of astronomical phenomena; the art of multiplying engravings; the introduction and improvement among us of all the important inventions of the Old World, are strikingly indicative of the progress of this country in the useful arts.

The net-work of railroads and telegraph lines by which this vast country is reticulated have not only developed its resources, but united emphatically, in metallic bands, all parts of the Union.

The hydraulic works of New York, Philadelphia, and Boston surpass in extent and importance those of ancient Rome.

But we have not confined our attention to the immediate application of science to the useful arts. We have entered the field of original research, and have enlarged the bounds of scientific knowledge.

Sixty years ago, besides the brilliant discoveries of Franklin in electricity, scarcely anything had been done among us in the way of original discovery. Our men of science were content with repeating the experiments and diffusing a knowledge of the discoveries of the learned of the Old World, without attempting to add a single new fact or principle to the existing stock. Within the last twenty-five or thirty years a remarkable improvement has taken place in this respect. Our natural history has been explored in all its branches; our geology has been investigated with results of the highest interest to practical and theoretical science. Discoveries have been made in pure chemistry and electricity which have received the approbation of the world. The advance which has been made in meteorology in this country, within the last twenty years, is equal to that made during the same period in all the world besides.

In 1793 there was not in the United States an instrument with which a good observation of the heavenly bodies could be made. There are now instruments at Washington, Cambridge, and Cincinnati equal to those at the best European observatories, and the original discoveries in astronomy within the last five years in this country are among the most brilliant of the age. I can hardly refrain from saying, in this connexion, that the "celestial mechanics" of La Place has been translated and extended by Bowditch.

Our knowledge of the geography and topography of the American continent has been rapidly extended by the labor and science of the officers of the United States army, and discoveries of much interest in distant seas have resulted from the enterprise of the navy.

In 1807 a survey of the coast of the United States was commenced, which at that time it was supposed no American was competent to direct. The work has, however, grown within the last few years, under a native superintendent, in importance and extent beyond any enterprise of the kind ever before attempted.

These facts conclusively prove that a great advance has been made among us, not only in the application of science to the wants of ordinary life, but to science itself, in its highest branches, in its adaptation to satisfy the cravings of the immortal mind.

In respect to literature, with the exception of some books of elementary education, and some theological treatises, of which scarcely any but those of Jonathan Edwards have any permanent value, and some works on local history and politics, like Hutchinson's Massachusetts, Jefferson's Notes on Virginia, the Federalist, Belknap's New Hampshire, and Morse's Geography, and a few others, America had not produced a single work of any repute in literature. We were almost wholly dependant on imported books. Even our Bibles and Testaments were, for the most part, printed abroad. The book trade is now one of the greatest branches of business, and many works of standard value and of high reputation in Europe as well as at home have been produced by American authors in every department of literary composition.

While the country has been expanding in dimensions, in numbers, and in wealth, the Government has applied a wise forecast in the adoption of measures necessary, when the world shall no longer be at peace, to maintain the national honor, whether by appropriate displays of vigor abroad, or by well adapted means of defence at home. A navy, which has so often illustrated our history by heroic achievements, though restrained in peaceful times in its operations to narrow limits, possesses, in its admirable elements, the means of great and sudden expansion, and is justly looked upon by the nation as the right arm of its power: an army, still smaller, but not less perfect in its detail, which has on many a field exhibited the military aptitudes and prowess of the race, and demonstrated the wisdom which has presided over its organization and government.

While the gradual and slow enlargement of these respective military arms has been regulated by a jealous watchfulness over the public treasure, there has, nevertheless, been freely given all that was needed to perfect their quality; and each affords the nucleus of any enlargement that the public exigencies may demand, from the millions of brave hearts and strong arms upon the land and water.

The navy is the active and aggressive element of national defence; and, let loose from our own seacoast, must display its power in the seas and channels of the enemy: to do this, it need not be large; and it can never be large enough to defend by its presence at home all our ports and harbors. But, in the absence of the navy, what can the regular army or the volunteer militia do against the enemy's line-of-battle ships and steamers, falling without notice upon our coast? What will guard our cities from tribute, our merchant vessels and our navy-yards from conflagration? Here, again, we see a wise forecast in the system of defensive measures, which, especially since the close of the war with Great Britain, has been steadily followed by our Government.

While the perils from which our great establishments had just escaped were yet fresh in remembrance, a system of fortifications was begun, which now, though not quite complete, fences in our important points with impassable strength. More than four thousand cannon may at any moment, within strong and permanent works, arranged with all the advantages and appliances that the art affords, be turned to the protection of the sea coast, and be served by the men whose hearths they shelter. Happy for us that it is so, since these are means of security that time alone can supply; and since the improvements of maritime warfare, by making distant expeditions easy and speedy, have made them more probable, and at the same time more difficult to anticipate and provide against. The cost of fortifying all the important points on our whole Atlantic and Gulf of Mexico frontier will not exceed the amount expended on the fortifications of Paris.

In this connexion one most important facility in the defence of the country is not to be overlooked; it is the almost instantaneous rapidity with which the soldiers of the army, and any number of the militia corps, may be brought to any point where a hostile attack may at any time be made or threatened.

And this extension of territory, embraced within the United States, increase of its population, commerce and manufactures, development of its resources by canals and railroads, and rapidity of intercommunication by means of steam and electricity, have all been accomplished without overthrow of or danger to the public liberties, by any assumption of military power; and, indeed, without any permanent increase of the army, except for the purpose of frontier defence, and of affording a slight guard to the public property; or of the navy, any further than to assure the navigator that, in whatsoever sea he shall sail his ship, he is protected by the stars and stripes of his country. And this, too, has been done without the shedding of a drop of blood, for treason or rebellion; while systems of popular representation have regularly been supported in the State Governments and in the General Government; while laws, national and State, of such a character have been passed, and have been so wisely administered, that I may stand up here to-day and declare, as I now do declare, in the face of all the intelligent of the age, that for the period which has elapsed, from the day that Washington laid the foundation of this Capitol to the present time, there has been no country upon earth in which life, liberty, and property have been more amply and steadily secured, or more freely enjoyed, than in these United States of America. Who is there that will deny this? Who is there prepared with a greater or a better example? Who is there that can stand upon the foundation of facts, acknowledged or proved, and assert that these our republican institutions have not answered the true ends of Government beyond all precedent in human history?

There is yet another view. There are still higher considerations. Man is an intellectual being, destined to immortality. There is a spirit in him, and the breath of the Almighty hath given him understanding. Then only is he tending toward his own destiny, while he seeks for knowledge or virtue, for the will of his Maker, and for just conceptions of his own duty. Of all important questions, therefore, let this, the most important of all, be first asked and first answered: in what country of the habitable globe, of great extent and large population, are the means of knowledge the most generally diffused and enjoyed among the people? This question admits of one, and only one, answer. It is here; it is here in these United States; it is among the descendants of those who settled at Jamestown; of those who were pilgrims on the shore of Plymouth; and of those other races of men, who, in subsequent times, have become joined in this great American family. Let one fact incapable of doubt or dispute satisfy every mind on this point. The population of the United States is 23,000,000. Now, take the map of the continent of Europe and spread it out before you. Take your scale and your dividers, and lay off in one area, in any shape you please, a triangle, square, circle, parallelogram, or trapezoid, and of an extent that shall contain 150,000,000 of people, and there will be found within the United States more persons who do habitually read and write than can be embraced within the lines of your demarcation.

But there is something even more than this. Man is not only an intellectual, but he is also a religious being, and his religious feelings and habits require cultivation.

Let the religious element in man's nature be neglected, let him be influenced by no higher motives than low self-interest, and subjected to no stronger restraint than the limits of civil authority, and he becomes the creature of selfish passions or blind fanaticism. The spectacle of a nation powerful and enlightened, but without christian faith, has been presented, almost within our own day, as a warning beacon for the nations.

On the other hand, the cultivation of the religious sentiment represses licentiousness, incites to general benevolence, and the practical acknowledgment of the brotherhood of man, inspires respect for law and order, and gives strength to the whole social fabric, at the same time that it conducts the human soul upward to the Author of its being.

Now, I think it may be stated with truth, in no country, in proportion to its population, are there so many benevolent establishments connected with religious instruction, Bible, Missionary, and Tract Societies, supported by public and private contributions, as in our own. There are also institutions for the education of the blind, of idiots, the deaf and dumb, the reception of orphan and destitute children, for moral reform, designed for children and females respectively; and institutions for the reformation of criminals, not to speak of those numerous establishments in almost every county and town in the United States for the reception of the aged, infirm, and destitute poor, many of whom have fled to our shores to escape the poverty and wretchedness of their condition at home.

In the United States there is no church establishment or ecclesiastical authority founded by Government. Public worship is maintained either by voluntary associations and contributions, or by trusts and donations of a charitable origin.

Now, I think it safe to say that a greater portion of the people of the United States attend public worship, decently clad, well behaved, and well seated, than of any other country of the civilized world.

Edifices of religion are seen every where. Their aggregate cost would amount to an immense sum of money. They are, in the general, kept in good repair, and consecrated to the purposes of public worship. In these edifices the people regularly assemble on the Sabbath day, which is sacredly set apart for rest by all classes from secular employment, and for religious meditation and worship, to listen to the reading of the Holy Scriptures, and discourses from pious ministers of the several denominations.

This attention to the wants of the intellect and of the soul, as manifested by the voluntary support of schools and colleges, of churches, and benevolent institutions, is one of the most remarkable characteristics of the American people, not less strikingly exhibited in the new than in the older settlements of the country.

On the spot where the first trees of the forest were felled, near the log cabins of the pioneers, are to be seen rising together the church and the school house. So has it been from the beginning, and God grant that it may thus continue!

"On other shores, above their mouldering towns,
In sullen pomp the tall cathedral frowns;
Simple and frail, our lowly temples throw
Their slender shadows on the paths below;
Scarce steal the winds, that sweep the woodland tracks,
The larch's perfume from the settler's axe,
'Ere, like a vision of the morning air,
His slight-framed steeple marks the house of prayer.
Yet Faith's pure hymn, beneath its shelter rude,
Breathes out as sweetly to the tangled wood,
As where the rays through blazing oriels pour
On marble shaft and tessellated floor.

Who does not admit that this unparalleled growth in prosperity and renown is the result, under Providence, of the Union of these States, under a general Constitution, which guaranties to each State a republican form of Government, and to every man the enjoyment of life, liberty, and the pursuit of happiness, free from civil tyranny or ecclesiastical domination?

And to bring home this idea to the present occasion, who does not feel that, when President Washington laid his hand on the foundation of the first Capitol building, he performed a great work of perpetuation of the Union and the Constitution? Who does not feel that this seat of the General Government, healthful in its situation, central in its position, near the mountains from whence gush springs of wonderful virtue, teeming with Nature's richest products, and yet not far from the bays and the great estuaries of the sea, easily accessible and generally agreeable in climate and association, does give strength to the Union of these States; that this city, bearing an immortal name, with its broad streets and avenues, its public squares and magnificent edifices of the General Government, erected for the purposes of carrying on within them the important business of the several Departments; for the reception of wonderful and curious inventions, the preservation of the records of American learning and genius; of extensive collections of the products of nature and art, brought hither for study and comparison from all parts of the world; adorned with numerous churches, and sprinkled over, I am happy to say, with many public schools, where all children of the city, without distinction, are provided with the means of obtaining a good education; where there are academies and colleges, professional schools and public libraries, should continue to receive, as it has heretofore received, the fostering care of Congress, and should be regarded as the permanent seat of the National Government. Here, too, a citizen of the great republic of letters, a republic which knows not the metes and bounds of political geography, has prophetically indicated his conviction that America is to exercise a wide and powerful influence in the intellectual world, by founding in this city, as a commanding position in the field of science and literature, and placing under the guardianship of the Government, an institution "for the increase and diffusion of knowledge among men."

With each succeeding year new interest is added to the spot; it becomes connected with all the historical associations of our country, with her statesmen and her orators, and, alas! its cemetery is annually enriched with the ashes of her chosen sons.

Before us is the broad and beautiful river, separating two of the original thirteen States, and which a late President, a man of de-

termined purpose and inflexible will, but patriotic heart, desired to span with arches of ever-enduring granite, symbolical of the firmly cemented union of the North and the South. That President was General Jackson.

On its banks repose the ashes of the Father of his Country, and at our side, by a singular felicity of position, overlooking the city which he designed, and which bears his name, rises to his memory the marble column, sublime in its simple grandeur, and fitly intended to reach a loftier height than any similar structure on the surface of the whole earth.

Let the votive offerings of his grateful countrymen be freely contributed to carry higher and still higher this monument. May I say, as on another occasion, "Let it rise; let it rise, till it meet the sun in his coming; let the earliest light of the morning gild it, and parting day linger and play on its summit!"

Fellow-citizens, what contemplations are awakened in our minds as we assemble here to re-enact a scene like that performed by WASHINGTON! Methinks I see his venerable form now before me, as presented in the glorious statue by Houdon, now in the capitol of Virginia. He is dignified and grave; but concern and anxiety seem to soften the lineaments of his countenance. The Government over which he presides is yet in the crisis of experiment. Not free from troubles at home, he sees the world in commotion and in arms all around him. He sees that imposing foreign Powers are half disposed to try the strength of the recently-established American Government. We perceive that mighty thoughts, mingled with fears as well as with hopes, are struggling within him. He heads a short procession over these then naked fields; he crosses yonder stream on a fallen tree; he ascends to the top of this eminence, whose original oaks of the forest stand as thick around him as if the spot had been devoted to Druidical worship, and here he performs the appointed duty of the day.

And now, fellow-citizens, if this vision were a reality; if Washington actually were now amongst us, and if he could draw around him the shades of the great public men of his own days, patriots and warriors, orators and statesmen, and were to address us in their presence, would he not say to us, "Ye men of this generation, I rejoice and thank God for being able to see that our

labors and toils and sacrifices were not in vain. You are prosperous, you are happy, you are grateful; the fire of liberty burns brightly and steadily in your hearts, while DUTY and the LAW restrain it from bursting forth in wild and destructive conflagration. Cherish liberty, as you love it; cherish its securities as you wish to preserve it. Maintain the Constitution which we labored so painfully to establish, and which has been to you such a source of inestimable blessings. Preserve the union of the States, cemented as it was by our prayers, our tears, and our blood. Be true to God, to your country, and to your duty. So shall the whole Eastern World follow the morning sun to contemplate you as a nation; so shall all generations honor you, as they honor us; and so shall that Almighty Power which so graciously protected us, and which now protects you, shower its everlasting blessings upon you and your posterity."

Great father of your country! we heed your words; we feel their force as if you now uttered them with lips of flesh and blood. Your example teaches us, your affectionate addresses teach us, your public life teaches us your sense of the value of the blessings of the Union. Those blessings our fathers have tasted, and we have tasted, and still taste. Nor do we intend that those who come after us shall be denied the same high fruition. Our honor as well as our happiness is concerned. We cannot, we dare not, we will not betray our sacred trust. We will not filch from posterity the treasure placed in our hands to be transmitted to other generations. The bow that gilds the clouds in the heavens, the pillars that uphold the firmament, may disappear and fall away in the hour appointed by the will of God; but until that day comes, or so long as our lives may last, no ruthless hand shall undermine that bright arch of Union and Liberty which spans the continent from Washington to California.

Fellow-citizens, we must sometimes be tolerant to folly, and patient at the sight of the extreme waywardness of men; but I confess that when I reflect on the renown of our past history, on our present prosperity and greatness, and on what the future hath yet to unfold; and when I see that there are men who can find in all this nothing good, nothing valuable, nothing truly glorious, I feel that all their reason has fled away from them, and left the entire control over their judgment and their actions to insanity and fanaticism ; and, more than all, fellow-citizens, if the purposes of fanatics and disunionists should be accomplished, the patriotic and intelligent of our generation would seek to hide themselves from the scorn of the world, and go about to find dishonorable graves.

Fellow-citizens, take *courage;* be of *good cheer.* We shall come to no such ignoble end. We shall live, and not die. During the period allotted to our several lives we shall continue to rejoice in the return of this Anniversary. The ill-omened sounds of fanaticism will be hushed; the ghastly spectres of *Secession* and *Disunion* will disappear, and the enemies of united constitutional liberty, if their hatred cannot be appeased, may prepare to sere their eyeballs as they behold the steady flight of the AMERICAN EAGLE, on his burnished wings, for years and years to come.

President FILLMORE, it is your singularly good fortune to perform an act such as that which the earliest of your predecessors performed fifty-eight years ago. You stand where he stood; you lay your hand on the corner-stone of a building designed greatly to extend that whose corner-stone he laid. Changed, changed is every thing around. The same sun, indeed, shone upon his head which now shines upon yours. The same broad river rolled at his feet, and bathes his last resting place, that now rolls at yours. But the site of this city was then mainly an open field. Streets and avenues have since been laid out and completed, squares and public grounds enclosed and ornamented, until the city which bears his name, although comparatively inconsiderable in numbers and wealth, has become quite fit to be the seat of government of a great and united people.

Sir, may the consequences of the duty which you perform so auspiciously to-day equal those which flowed from his act. Nor this only; may the principles of your administration, and the wisdom of your political conduct, be such as that the world of the present day, and all history hereafter, may be at no loss to perceive what example you have made your study.

Fellow-citizens, I now bring this address to a close, by expressing to you, in the words of the great Roman orator, the deepest wish of my heart, and which I know dwells deeply in the hearts of all who hear me: "Duo modó haec opto; unum, UT MORIENS 'POPULUM ROMANUM LIBERUM RELINQUAM; hoc mihi majus a diis im-

'mortalibus dari nihil potest: alterum, ut ita cuique eveniat, ut 'de republicâ quisque mereatur."

And now, fellow-citizens, with hearts void of hatred, envy, and malice towards our own countrymen, or any of them, or towards the subjects or citizens of other Governments, or towards any member of the great family of man; but exulting, nevertheless, in our own peace, security, and happiness, in the grateful remembrance of the past, and the glorious hopes of the future, let us return to our homes, and with all humility and devotion offer our thanks to the Father of all our mercies, political, social, and religious.

www.ingramcontent.com/pod-product-compliance
Lightning Source LLC
LaVergne TN
LVHW020742120826
845150LV00010B/2359
9781418193584